New York:
A FEAST OF MEMORIES

DAVID DONALD CARROLL

Skyward Publishing

Skyward Publishing
P.O. Box 40209
Memphis, TN 38174-40209

First Edition

ISBN: 1-881-554-01-5
Library of Congress Catalog Number: 92-061110

Acknowledgments

The writer happily concedes that the earliest influence in the creation of this book came from a longtime friend, Virginia's nationally known poet, Mrs. Margaret Ward Morland, to whom he happily and deservedly grants sincerest credit. He adds that she played no part in the volume's composition and therefore does not share any culpability for its publication.

The author acknowledges the endless clerical aid and unbelievable patience of Mrs. Charlene Moore; also the arduous hours of reading aloud by Mrs. Ella ("Tot") Phelan Weems in order to give the author a fresh perspective; the talented contributions of Mrs. Marcia Wiley Casey who, over a several year period, weathered all the author's rocky moods. The author is indebted to Mrs. Phyllis Tickle, Mrs. Margaret Ward Morland, Miss Charlotte Schultz and Mrs. Miriam Northrop for all the tedious hours of proofreading, as well as their experienced and excellent counsel and to Billy Price Carroll, widely recognized for her paintings — especially portraits. A few of her pen and ink sketches appear in this book.

Lastly, the author acknowledges the conjugal guidance of Billy Price Carroll whose tolerance proved the hardihood of their marriage. He says without her, all credits to him would have been post-mortem.

Honoraria

Worthy reader, have you ever pondered the heroes of olden New York — back then, now, perchance tomorrow; in short, the lives of the uniformed or non-uniformed strivers who seldom win the barest thanks — indeed, even public notice?

Herein are the men and rare women who have waged, won, and yet still bear our battles against savage human force and Earth's primal elements. This reference, of course, is to policemen, firemen, chemical and disaster crews, medical frontiersmen, rescue squads, handlers of noxious substances, and others. These are the men and women whose families pay the human cost of guarding yours and mine.

Who among us can say he or she has truly glimpsed new or old New York unless such a viewer has experienced the risk and sometimes loss which these imperiled lives endure?

Money pays the cost but hearts bear the loss.

To New York City:
A Scream in the Night

What was this author's first contact with New York City? A gift-trip by his parents as his high school graduation present in 1924.

Because he lacked a travel case, an older sister lent him her own. When he boarded a ship sailing from Charleston, SC to New York, he was promptly assigned to a cabin containing two passenger bunks. He liked the adventure of not knowing what kind of man his cabin mate might prove to be.

Being then a college-minded young man, he did not return to his cabin until late night, so fascinating were the deck views and other passengers.

Retiring finally to his ship quarters, he did not turn on the light since his cabin mate was asleep. When he accidentally touched his fellow traveler's clothing in the dark, he suddenly realized it was all silk fabric — indeed, women's lingerie! Shocked and terrified, he audibly gasped as he heard a piercing feminine scream, not once but several times. With groping and bumbling awkwardness he felt his way to the cabin door and dashed out.

Meanwhile, other male passengers were out in the hall in their bed clothing, some of them bearing walking canes as clubs to deal with the scoundrel molesting a woman passenger. The ship's master, speeding to the scene, quieted down the belligerent male passengers and finally placed the author in a vacant cabin.

This misadventure made the young male passenger remain out of sight until the uproar quieted. He was eager to disembark without any efforts at explanation, innocent though he was - utterly innocent.

Dedicated to my wife and (late) parents.

Statue of Liberty

Prelude

You mean my olden, golden New York —
Provider of the unobtainable,
Lurer to the unattainable?
A cask of memories you uncork:

Foreword

New York: A Feast of Memories proffers moods, motivations and activities.

These recollections and reminiscences are prompted by the author's super-annuated mischief.

A Re-Sampling of Times Past

Table of Contents

1   An Array of Memories
2   Courtship and Comedown
3   When Mortal Stars Cease to Shine
5   New York Potpourri
7   A City Full of Pride and Enterprise
8   Where Honesty and Quality Were the Golden Policy
9   Stages for Actors of All Ages
10   Manhattan Mirror
11   Dance, Song and Chance
13   When Ladies Whoop for Single Bed
15   A Bridge to Glory
16   The Golden Past Before Our Brassy Present
17   The Boy-Joy in a Man
19   Old Friends from Old Places
20   Ponder the Imponderable
21   King Barnum and Some Royal Georges
22   The Lofty Heights of New York
23   How a Losing Champion Died Undefeated
25   America in Review
26   Swinging Tables
27   How Beat the Hearts of Gotham
28   Smile the While You Hide Your Guile
29   The Dearest Way That Wars Live On
30   A Gust of Wartime Memories
31   How to Get a New York Bank Loan
33   Champions in Sky, Water, and on Stage
34   The Reformed Warrior
35   The Scramble Up — The Scramble Down
36   Conquest and Calamity
37   When Brothers, Even Books, Go to War
39   Why New York, Stranger?

continued

40	A Seer Who Spoke Then and the Slain Who Speak Forever
41	When War Rages, Cupid Ages
42	Unsung Masters
43	Dockside Men and Verbal Sin
44	Ants in Pants Beneath the Sky
45	On Foreign Relations
46	A Chicken-Hearted Fish Fancier
47	Of Squalor and the Dollar
49	New York Versus a Hometown Block
50	A Queen's Humiliation
51	Human War's Most Inhuman Plot
52	New York Hotels Are Stages Too
53	Requiem and Travel Ticket
54	Age May Tell but Must Not Toll
55	Inventory of Men and Means
57	When Johnny Came Sailing, Whooping Home
59	A Stronghold of Loveliness and Capability
60	A People's Armistice
61	The Nation's Capital for Selling
63	Holy Light and Darkest Night
64	Devious Paths of Human Quest
65	Faith Is Not a Wraith
67	The Great Human Roundup
69	The Learning Venture, Youth's Adventure
70	The Drum and Fife of Youthful Life
71	Children, Pre-TV
72	Whence Comes Great Music?
73	Crosscurrents of Life
74	Rebound
75	While the People Sleep
76	A Tardy Truth for Men
77	Urban Thrall

Pen and Ink Sketches

Prelude	Statue of Liberty
4	Resting
6	Central Park
12	Subway
14	Brooklyn Bridge
18	Organ Grinder
24	Flatiron Building
32	East End of the Island
38	Grand Central Railway Station
48	Residences of a Past Era
56	Double-Decker Buses
58	Park Avenue
62	The Cloisters
66	Downtown View
68	At the Museum
78	Trinity Church at the Foot of Wall Street

Sketches by Billy Price Carroll

An Array of Memories

Broadway shows, Fulton markets,
Radio City, leggy Rockettes;
Macy's Parade, and street debaters.
Great libraries, singing waiters;
Romantic Staten Island Ferry,
A restful trip, often merry;
Homebound folk in Penn Station,
Loving Christmas organ's celebration.

Courtship and Comedown

Pushcart garment trucks on Seventh Avenue —
Oy, oy and enjoy!
To rise from Standing Room Only tickets
To boxes at the Met
Was quite a social run;
Also Easter breakfast at the Plaza, lunch at "21";
Foods for taste and fun were often found
In murky lure of Chinatown.
And in Rockefeller Plaza
To give a first-time date special zoom,
You offered her cocktails and rapture-views
From the sky-high Rainbow Room —
But come the Great Depression
Eating at the Automat was where It Was At . . . .

When Mortal Stars Cease to Shine

Among the pangs of New York,
Nineteen forty-two, fifty-four and fifty-nine,
Three Barrymore events
Made many hearts sincerely pine:
Ethel, John, and Lionel saw Death's curtain fall,
Thus ending theater's royal trinity —
The brightest one of all.

Resting

New York Potpourri

The tourists sure to gawp and gather
At Rockefeller Plaza;
The taxidrivers braving heat or mayhap sleet,
Pontificating on public ills
With judgments overneat;
The Greenwich Village bagels
Served by day or night;
The furtive, low-voiced beggars there,
Oft-time free of any plight.

Central Park

A City Full of Pride and Enterprise

A Central Park outing, food at Tavern On The Green,
Could bring you happy boating with a Southern Queen.
A car? Police would seldom let you park it
Near monied bank or diamond market;
Newcomers bent astonished looks
On costly suits flatstacked in piles at Brooks';
But Stock Exchange and brokers' shouts
Bestirred in tourists nervous doubts.
The Empire State skyscraper opened in the Depression,
But how its nighttime tower view undid a maid's discretion!

Where Honesty and Quality Were the Golden Policy

John Wanamaker, Franklin Simon, Altman's,
Abercrombie & Fitch,
Macy's, Gimbel's, Sak's Fifth Avenue,
Bonwit Teller, Lord and Taylor,
All struck it rich.
So what's the lesson to the world?
That winners never lowered standards
Despite the tempting money swirl.

Stages for Actors of All Ages

New York became a host to budding magazines,
And "Mademoiselle" raised girls to queens,
While one starring Bryn Mawr Miss
Added ten fine editorships to her list.
And Radio City's dancing, prancing
Feats and treats upon its stages
Drew gaping, motley folk of all ages.
But comics past all human price
Were safely padded little kiddies
Battling wayward skates on ice.

Manhattan Mirror

At Times Square, see hometown newspapers
Assembled rack on rack;
Dispatriated readers there
Vainly seeking "auld lang syne's" contact.
Fifth Avenue storewindows
Designed to enthrall;
Irish, Polish, Easter Parades,
The biggest struts of all!
Walt Disney's all-age Mickey Mouse giant balloon
Afloat just overhead —
The kind of day that no good parent
Ever spent in bed!

Dance, Song and Chance

Irene and Vernon Castle made of dance a rhythm-romance,
While dancing "flappers", spreading the "Charleston" craze,
Romped and wriggled madcap ways.
The haunting, olden wartime songs lingered on,
But when the Wall Street markets crashed, 1929,
A golden land turned bleak and saturnine.
Will that time ever come again?
The answer ever is:
If conscience goes, will there be sin?
Does folly flourish without men?

Subway

When Ladies Whoop for Single Bed

But these vignettes of New York City
Should also sound a note of comic pity
For the knee-sore scrubwomen on the daybreak subway
Going home to Jersey hubby.
They often guffawed, whooped, and claimed at home
A soundly sleeping and (they hoped and said)
A nonromantic hubby in a separate bed.
Is this the tattling of a snooper?
No, every lady was a whooper.

"*Brooklyn Bridge*"

A Bridge to Glory

(Opened in 1883)

Oh, Brooklyn Bridge!
That phantom dream bewrought in steel
To wed the earth unto the sky;
That spirit vaulting limits real
With science boggling mind and eye!
But stricken hero-architect,
Directing from your nearby window,
Did you not uncounted times reflect
Upon the human cost of mortal splendor?

The Golden Past Before Our Brassy Present

Know you olden New York waterside batteries' lure?
There was a time when voice, water, and romance
Charmed folk with seaside music and air's blend
As hearts were won by songs of matchless Jenny Lind.

The Boy-Joy in a Man

In this century's first half,
New York, as if to play a prank upon itself,
Kept sturdy, odd old structures
Standing here and there beside great towers.
It seemed a bit of wilful hodgepodge
That argued realtors shared a human yen
To keep as men some things they loved as boys.
Of course, a pipe dream —
But is there fitter human joy
Than manhood gently bound to boy?

Organic Grinder

Old Friends from Old Places

In early century years, many articles of utility
Linked Gotham to the nation's smallest towns:
Potbellied stoves, old clocks and gardens —
Such old friends bespoke city, town, and farm's amiability,
With barber poles, hitching posts,
Street organs, spittoons all around.
How dear today are old-time things and parts
Which starred in times when human hearts
Were fired not by monied notability
But by human empathy and gentility!

Ponder the Imponderable

If you should live some years in New York
Think not to learn the city
By short-lived forays here and there;
Nor yet to shuck it off
By going home somewhere.
For if you once invest your life
Within the contrarieties
Of multi-father'd Gotham —
Where oceans, rivers, land, and buildings
Have fused with folk, time, and light
To form a world, but not unto itself —
Then indeed, reflect on this:
To learn New York within a lifetime's spin
Is to biograph Methuselah
On a single weekend.

King Barnum and Some Royal Georges

In that era
P. T. Barnum's showman spirit fired New York's Hippodrome,
While riverboats and ocean liners bade you roam;
England had its sovereign Georges wearing royal crown,
But New York also had a few in town
Like George Abbott, George Burns, and George S. Kaufman,
Each an institution
Repelling age restraints with hardy constitution.

The Lofty Heights of New York

Greatness in New York, as some folk thought,
Was best expressed not by
Ablest Broadway oligarchs
But by museums, dramas, also concerts in the park.
Few events can fuel human ire
Like New York drama born of fire,
Nor warm the cockles of a fulsome heart
Like favorite actors in some touching part.
And did you ever know the thrill
Of seeing a prima ballerina dance to music's will?
Did you oft attend the Metropolitan Opera on opening night
With its glitter, glamour, and voices reaching magic height?
Or heard the New York Philharmonic orchestra play?
Ah, what a life when senses hold all sway.

How a Losing Champion Died Undefeated

One hero in this century's early years
Should prove a brace to us of later times;
Irish John L. Sullivan, world champion bare fist boxer,
Proved himself a matchless drinker
By downing nonstop liquor-filled glasses.
In later years he became a derelict
Until one day, dethroned, he poured out his glass to vow,
And later prove 'til death, 'twas said,
His bone-dry leadership in a war
To stay the loss of other men to drink.
Why cite this prideful man who suffered pain replete?
To show that New York life is indeed
A two-way street.

The Flatiron Building

America in Review

'Twas quite a thing in our century's early years
For European kin to judge New York with jeers.
Quite truly, our foreign cousins at the least
Must have gazed and gaped to find us offspring
No longer forced to cope with wilderness and beast,
But proving pelf's the way to highest rank
As we romped both to and from the bank.
What mainly raised New York and America
To richly monied commonweal?
You know — inventions and swapping the noble horse
For the mile-conquering, money-minting automobile.

Swinging Tables

Two nightclub ladies ruled in different ways:
Songstress Texas Guinan whooped atop a table
Greeting men, "Hello, sucker," just for fun,
While winsome table-topper Helen Morgan
Sang mellowed, tender songs that also won.

How Beat the Hearts of Gotham?

If need cried out,
Did Gothamites lend their aid?
Oh yes, though lack of time to stop
Might some good folk dissuade;
But New York life confirmed a truthful text:
"To Fate's dread call, no one knows who's next."

Smile the While You Hide Your Guile

For ladies full of nixes
You proffered cocktails at the Top of the Sixes
Or Rodin's statue named "The Kiss," at Metropolitan Museum
And lunch beside the pool.
Enough delirium in New York
To keep a man a fool!

The Dearest Ways That Wars Live On

New York always was a songwriters' mall,
And World War I induced a bittersweet interlude.
Do you recall
These heart-snatching cues
From that War's music hall?
"Over There, Over There;"
"It's Apple Blossom Time in Normandy;"
"Smile the While You Bid Me Sad Adieu;"
"Good-bye, Picadilly, Farewell, Leicester Square;"
And "Johnny, Get Your Gun, Get Your Gun!"
Ah, what a web of memories
Those poignant songs have spun!

A Gust of Wartime Memories

Gotham's Roaring Twenties were heirs of World War I,
But wars always shape more lives than deaths:
Thus wartime jobs brought Southern blacks up North,
While unions grew with labor's giddy power climb,
And purblind Prohibition spawned both gangs and crime,
While wartime aviation opened skies to worldwide trade,
As mortal combat boomed medical science and prosthetic aid.
Thus human loss brought grisly profit-gain.

How to Get a New York Bank Loan

A young Southern business man,
While lugging a long, heavy travel trunk,
During his Penn Station arrival in New York
Was watching a queenly, unknown belle nearby
And bumped his lengthy trunk a third time
Into the legs of a grumbling, same-sized young male.
The latter slugged the Southerner with a fist holding steel keys,
Thus cutting ugly, bleeding gashes in the girl-watcher's forehead.
The South-born rebel answered with a blow,
Causing the first slugger to fall
And strike steel-ribbed steps with his head,
Apparently leaving him stone dead!
Having seen Sing Sing prison on a tour there,
The wretched Southerner visioned ghastly years in jail.
The angel porters and fervid prayer raised the mute man up
To grin at his bloody, gashed target,
Both men gleefully gripping hands and slapping backs.
The Southerner rushed directly to his appointment
Where the vice-president bank czar proffered first-time praise
And growled: "We like scrappy clients, they're never slack,
They collect their own accounts and pay our money back."

*East End
of the Island*

Champions in Sky, Water, and on Stage

Early in this century,
With rope a-twirling, wit a-swirling,
Cowboy Will Rogers starred on New York stage;
And Brooklyn's young daughter, Gertrude Ederle,
Was first female to swim the awesome English Channel —
Ah, young hearties, what a golden age!

. . . .

But in 1937, Amelia Earhart, the sky's own darling,
How flew you into wordless, starkest mystery?

The Reformed Warrior

Know you the greatest, noblest lady
Associated with New York?
Her fame defies a common name,
For she's the statue to all liberty here found,
Looking toward Europe's endless battleground.

One returning American soldier,
Worn out by the First World War,
Expressed a thought battle-wrought
And based on reason sound:
"Lady Liberty," he said: "If you ever look at me again,
You'll shore Lord have to turn around."

The Scramble Up — The Scramble Down

Gotham students, readers,
Know well how best to spend;
Fourth Avenue would let you choose
From wondrous books already used;
And skimpers found a blessing
In cheap, quick snacks, thanks to delicatessen.
Street vendors briskly sold it — you name it —
Anywhere they proclaimed it,
While shoeshine lads with rare personality
Got rich men's tips on the market.
But come the nation's madcap crash October 1929,
Some once-rich brokers envied profits
Earned by lusty, cheerful shoeshine boys,
So fickle is this vale of pain and joy.

Conquest and Calamity

In the year 1927,
The first transatlantic flight by Charles Lindbergh
(From New York to Paris)
Made New York a hero's capital.
Gotham's people brooked no curb of joy
For the modest, shy young conqueror
Of the vast ocean, weather, solitude,
Also fatigue and technology,
Plus unsought, unrelenting national limelight.
On landing later in England,
He humbly proffered to airport folk his name,
But overnight the world had already hailed his fame.

. . . .

For parents Anne and Charles, the cost of glory?
Alas, you know the Lindbergh infant's tragic story.

When Brothers, Even Books, Go to War

Consider the mind-boggling entity named New York City,
Itself the world's greatest commerce and finance center;
The publications and news crossroads;
Also largest harbor, foremost airways, railroads,
Indeed the greatest focus of communication.
In that New York, der Fuehrer faced a City-Nation.
How traced we German atom secrets, new and scary?
Why, my friend, we did it partly in
The New York Public Library!

Grand Central
Station

Why New York, Stranger?

What think you brings so many folk to Gotham?
A will to leave behind small places' social chores
To join an ethos drawn from many shores.
Thus Main Street and County Fairs,
With static outlook, sometimes family strain,
Oft sent to New York untold human gain;
For in the city many find new equanimity
Because they love the peace
Of the Big Apple's social anonymity.

A Seer Who Spoke Then and the Slain Who Speak Forever

During World War II, Gotham's Harvard Club steambaths
Rested H. V. Kaltenborn from radioing Hitler's wraths.
Folk did not remark to him how his words exploring peace
Did not bespeak the future's destined choice.
The war did come, and in the Club's greatest hall
Could be sadly seen upon the wall
The metal-wrought names of Harvard's noble dead.

When War Rages, Cupid Ages

World War II naval service in New York
Brought insights of a ghastly kind —
Called "The Manhattan Project."
During huge war-buying operations
We never knew till Fate had tolled the knell
That our buying duties bought atomic bombs invoking Hell.
No anodyne . . . no anodyne.
In Satan's infernal lexicon
It might be listed as The Mad-Hatin' Project.
But now in retrospect it seems
Both sad and much awry
That Time best recalls
The lovely girls at hotel's wartime officer's balls.

Unsung Masters

But if you wished to see the skill
Which shaped machines with which to build,
You sought high up, under rafters,
The European steel machine-crafters
Who shifted work from craftsmen's handwrought pride
To factory volume, teeming far and wide.
Ah, New York, your wealth and brain
Have wrought from massive stone and steel
The speed and money-based barriers all men feel.

Dockside Men and Verbal Sin

Saw you ever New York's waterfront
Where tugboats' life was pull and shove?
(You couldn't listen to the dockhands' language, Aunt Sue.)
Today the human sweat and strain
Of dockside labor isn't still a bane.
Now motorized equipment proffers little huff and guff,
Thus proving that it wasn't all that cussin'
Which moved the heavy stuff.

Ants in Pants Beneath the Sky

Ascend New York's skymost rooftops
Soaring breathless high.
Peek down their startling canyons,
Where tiny insects run awry.
Then realize aghast, my friend,
Those tiny insects are you and I!

On Foreign Relations

For New York insights into European fun,
You teamed up with a foreign lad or lass
Who's in a club where each may bring someone.
Take care — our Yankee standards may seem crass:
Don't try to climb another culture on the run.

. . . .

But learning when to creep or leap —
That's half the bloomin' fun.

A Chicken-Hearted Fish Fancier

One oft unsung but kingly dish
In New York's countless dining places
Was fresh-caught tasty, varied fish
Fetched in from nigh or distant fishing spaces.
One eastside dining spot said on its wall,
"The fish you eat today
Slept last night in Chesapeake Bay."
A dining, reading Southern bloke
Somehow always felt a sense of sin;
Regarding fish
He deemed it nice to learn
Just where the oceans grow them,
But eating them, glad he was
He didn't personally know them.

Of Squalor and the Dollar

In a time of earnings scant and low,
The '30's brought to Gotham hordes from Puerto Rico,
Also "wall art" illustrating sordid life
Seen worldwide when want is rife.
How sad that folk must always flee
One of life's worst jailers, poverty;
But who among us now shows care
For how life's problem-bearers fare?
Unless a man's own ox is gored,
What cares he for the bloodied horde?
Or do we rally against an evil
Only when it costs us —
Like the cotton boll weevil?

Residences of a Past Era

New York Versus a Hometown Block

New York drew a nation's keenest minds
From other places, other climes;
But reader, pause and ponder:
There are tempting choices here and yonder.
Which would you rather be —
A single New York financial czar
Or a member of five successive generations
Of bankers, writers, lawyers at the bar —
All drawn from one Southern small-town block?
What a tribe and not a one in hock!

A Queen's Humiliation

In 1943 the pride of ravaged, wartime France,
The titan ocean liner, "Normandie" by name,
Used as largest troopship,
Burned at New York's shorebound dock
And workmen's blunder bore the blame.
How great the wound to human pride
When noble, ocean-bound ambition
Sinks at foreign landlubber's dockside!

Human War's Most Inhuman Plot

New York's stubby Mayor LaGuardia showed dual genius,
Reading Sunday comic sheets to war-shadowed children,
Yet serving ultra-honestly the Nation's cause.
New York became a network of World War II intrigue,
As its mayor, public library, Columbia University,
And Staten Island buildings played atomic weapon roles,
Known only to the nation's topmost leadership,
Employing Satan's guile to serve our Christian goals.

. . . .

How strangely we do serve His will
By plotting best the ways to kill!

New York Hotels Are Stages Too

Fine hotels can polarize alien personalities
Or mayhap show what you really are
By your quaffing, laughing, musing in the hotel bar.
Ah, yes, hotels form the meeting place
Of crassest goals or social grace.
The names of Gotham's lordly, plush hotels, you ask?
You miss the point, my friend:
The hotel lobbies of all great cities
Are where human drama, seen and unseen, lives.

. . . .

Why, some good folk (though less discreet)
Just stop in
To rest their aching feet!

Requiem and Travel Ticket

New York is sought as a sure-cure center
For folk whose springtime hearts
Have turned to ice-cold winter —
But what of lovers quickly wed by Gotham marriage?
Some may find that rustic faith
Rides ill in gilded carriage.
To lose one's mate means long to bleed;
And to show vain grief proves head in need.
But beauty truly loved never dies;
It only moves to live in other eyes.

Age May Tell but Must Not Toll

Do worried parents fear
That Gotham ill-shapes the young of age?
Accept the word of a onetime lad, now a druid sage:
What we've done to dodge our duty
Will cost our youths some pristine beauty.
Fear we now that modern youths' "me-first" mind
Will bring to them, with graying hair,
The sorrow caused by hungry soul
When life's cupboard grows bare?
Think we that youths have lost all sense of goal?
Ah, my life-mates yet alive,
Our own delusion, bearing dread of Fate,
Is all that makes us old
And not the calendar's change of date.

Inventory of Men and Means

Financial genius starring in a realm of chance?
Gotham was a world leader in high finance.
Need of armed force to keep the peace of night or day?
New York police were second only to the Army, USA.
Want to ride the busiest, best run railroad?
Gotham subways bore the greatest human load.
City theaters packed 'em in like farm potatoes.
And if you sinned and fell from ardent faith,
New York offered chapels full of saving grace —
But humanwrought, many churches bore
The bane of sometimes empty space.

Double-Decker Buses

When Johnny Came Sailing, Whooping Home

In 1945, joyous pandemonium at Times Square
When peace ended World War II —
And kinfolk later greeted troopships home again,
Praise Jesu!
Ah, then New Yorkers saw returned servicemen enjoy
The vaulted ceilings, human swirl
At Grand Central Station.
But humanizing all of life for Easter night,
The Holy Grace of candlelight
Shone forth Saint Patrick's grateful consecration.

Park Avenue

A Stronghold of Loveliness and Capability

To see female America at her lovely best
You only had to wait
For your upstairs-dressing date
While your eyes went a-swimmin'
In the lobby of The Barbizon for Women.
But no smart girl upstairs primping
Would keep you long downstairs waiting
With all that lobby competition sassy-baiting.

A People's Armistice

Mayhap one supernal gain may come
From Gotham's mingling worldwide peoples,
Thus bringing deeper human insight
Into hearthside dreams and hopes
Beyond the reach of world leaders, even Popes;
Thereby may end the brash irrationalities,
Thus plucking from oblivion's brink
This planet, threatened now by nuclear fatalities —
A time so lunatic to sober folk who think!

The Nation's Capital for Selling

New York foremostly is a money-making city;
But in the hurly-burly of the dollar chase
And the ever rising torment of the telephone,
Whence came some warmth in business interchange?
The answer:
At mid-day lunch, sunset cocktail hour, and dinner date,
Mayhap garnished by Broadway theater set to music;
Or by late night bingers softening over-canny buyers —
All conceived for Mammon's holy cause of selling —
For lack of which all bosses and directors fall to yelling.

The Cloisters

Holy Light and Darkest Night

In 1965 New York received the gracious Light
Of His Holiness, Pope Paul VI.
But at the year's end, the city suffered blackest dark
As Gotham lights and power failed by human fault.
Ink-black night then reigned supreme.
All city life became full weird,
But many cherished that eerie time
When Gotham life was locked in peace sublime!

Devious Paths of Human Quest

At Gotham's sumptuous stores
The rich betook their choice.
(I say a weakling's way to keep a woman in good voice.)
After theater, on to Reuben's for its magic sandwiches,
With cordial spirit there unfeigned by sons of riches.
At Columbia University, also N.Y.U.,
Talent oft to genius grew;
And there a smalltown girl, with love Victorian,
Could (and did) win a future-great historian.

Faith Is Not a Wraith

Know you New York's unique faiths?
Seek out a meeting of the Quaker Friends
And you'll not mind the lack of music —
    It sings where human spirits blend.
Catholics? Hear the Roman and the Greek
With music welling from a Russian basso,
And note the sacred, scholar'd orthodoxy
    Of Jews whose cruel suffering
    Never was, or is, by proxy.
Indeed, scan the scope of many creeds —
Manhattan proffers evermuch
To mortals' lonely, endless needs.

Downtown View

The Great Human Roundup

Sometimes, to hear Gotham folk whoop and holler,
You'd never deem its ruler the silent dollar.
But anyone who poses as New York's definer
Would promise you, in a rice bowl, all of China.
Judge not New York as a city of the world —
It is instead
A world within a city.

At the Museum

The Learning Venture, Youth's Adventure

In its hostess roles, New York could play romantic parts.
All America (but mainly Eastern, Southern states)
Often found the city a matchmaker for younger hearts,
One offering great adventure at low excursion rates.
Thus jobs, studies, enterprises brought newcomers
Seeking moonlight on the Hudson, life's theater everywhere
With minds and hearts in interchange —
When such allurements offer, what's for youth or age to fear?

The Drum and Fife of Youthful Life

Gotham's sex books raised a lusty clamor
When Kathleen Windsor wrote "Forever Amber,"
But tender songs best bespoke
The things between a girl and bloke.
Do New York summer schools proffer more than books?
Yes indeed, many lads learn the most
When Cupid plays the role of host.
The greatest feat of any university
Is bonding truth to minds' diversity.

Children, Pre-TV

In olden Gotham, children taxed your brain and eye,
Asking questions, why on why;
But now, where has fled their birthright joy
Of feeling all of life is just their toy?
My friend,
The answer is (and what a sin!)
That now most children find more glee
In gapes or yips and howls
At T.V.
But the little imp, his sister too,
Still jab a mental fork,
Asking questions on a crowded bus
In New York.

Whence Comes Great Music?

New York drew music from a nation on a spree.
Of course giant cities don't create true melody —
For doesn't it arise from tones of fervid lives
Transformed by basic chords of humankind?
But how music's mortal names
Could fill and thrill the greatest music halls!

Crosscurrents of Life

Underlying the vast allness of New York
Were and are its many-toned hotels
Where oft the human pulse of Gotham dwells:
For in their lobbies come the sudden cries
For old friends recognized,
With clasp of arms and grip of palms again.
Also expectant moments bringing rich reunion,
Betimes the radiant aura of a friendship just begun.
Ah, thus could end years of solitude or separation.

Rebound

What makes New York a place
That sets a grieving heart upon a healing spree?
Why, friend, have you never sought in life a second chance?
And if you have,
Did you ever find a better place than Gotham
To discard the dreary shroud of lost romance?

While the People Sleep

New York's governors, mayors through the years
Were oft more skilled than their national peers.
But what's the aim of average politicians?
Does not the very thought excite suspicions?
The outcome could be worse than costly —
What official heeds the need of folk's protection
When he's "home-free" again
After re-election?

A Tardy Truth for Men

Who were and are unmonumented heroes of New York?
The unsung secretaries binding boss to work;
They it was (and is) who know the records,
Check the facts,
And seldom do they earn discharge's axe.
Without them, fellowmen, there would not be a you or I,
So let us males belay our bellowing —
From man's original birth
The first hero was a heroine.

Urban Thrall

The risk of mortal crush
In subways' doomsday rush;
The greatest lark —
In which park? Central, Gramercy, day or dark?
The light that never failed
In Metropolitan Life's great tower;
The surge of daily newspaper trucks
Conveying printed power;
The Lewisohn-Goldman open-air concerts;
And famous old world Carnegie Hall,
Where genius gained its just deserts
And proved the magic of it all!

Trinity Church at the Foot of Wall Street

Index

A

Abbott, George 21
Abercrombie and Fitch 8
Altman, B. 8
Army, USA 55
atomic bombs 41
Automat 2
automobile 25

B

bagels 5
bank 25
bank czar 31
bank, monied 7
bankers 49
barber poles 19
Barbizon for Women 59
Barnum, P. T. 21
Barrymore, Ethel, John, Lionel 3
battery 16
beggars 5
books 35
Bonwit Teller 8
boxes at the Met 2
Broadway shows 1
Broadway theater 61
brokers 35
Brooklyn Bridge 15
Brooks(store for men) 7
Bryn Mawr 9
Burns, George 21

C

Carnegie Hall 78
Catholics 65
Central Park 7, 78
China 67
Chinatown 2

Chesapeake Bay 46
Christmas organs 1
City-Nation, der Fuehrer, German 37
Columbia University 51, 64
concerts, Lewisohn-Goldman 78
concerts 22
County Fairs 39

D

Depression 2, 7
delicatessen 35
diamond market 7
Disney, Walt 10

E

Earhart, Amelia 33
Easter Parade 10
Ederle, Gertrude 33
Empire State Building 7
English Channel 33
European steel machine-crafters 42

F

Ferry, Staten Island 1
Fifth Avenue 10
"Forever Amber" 70
Fourth Avenue 35
Franklin Simon 8
Fulton Market 1

G

garment trucks 2
Gimbels 8
Gotham 67
Gramercy Park 78
Grand Central Station 57

great libraries 1
Greek 65
Greenwich Village 5
Guinan, Texas 26

H

Harvard Club 40
Hippodrome, P. T. Barnam's 21
hitching posts 19
Hitler 40
horse 25
hotels 52, 73
Hudson River 69

I

inventions 25
Irish Parades 10

J

Jersey 13
Jews 65
John Wanamaker 8

K

Kaltenborn, H.V. 40
Kaufman, George S. 21
knee-sore scrubwomen 13

L

LaGuardia, Fiorello, Mayor 51
lawyers 49
Lewisohn-Goldman open air concerts 78
Lind, Jenny 16
Lindberg, Charles and Anne 36
Lord and Taylor 8

M

Macy's 8
Macy's parade 1
Mademoiselle magazine 9
magazines 9
Manhattan Project 41
manhood/boyhood 17
Methuselah 20
Metropolitan Life's Tower 78
Metropolitan Museum 22, 28
Metropolitan Opera 2, 22
Mickey Mouse balloon 10
Morgan, Helen 26
museums 22

N

newspapers 10
newspaper trucks 78
New York batteries' lure 16
nonromantic hubby 13
"Normandie," French ocean liner 50

O

ocean liners 21
old clocks 19
old-time things and parts 19
orchestra 22

P

parades 10
Penn Station 1
Plaza Hotel, Easter breakfast at 2
Polish Parade 10
Popes 60
Pope Paul VI, His Holiness 63
potbellied stove 19
prima ballerina 22
Prohibition 30
public library 51
Puerto Rico 47
pushcart garment truck 2

Q

Quaker Friends 65

R

Radio City 1, 9
Rainbow Room 2
Reuben's restaurant 64
Rockefeller Plaza 2, 5
Rockettes 1
Rodin, Auguste 28
Rogers, Will 33
Roman 65
Russian basso 65

S

Saint Patrick's Cathedral 57
Sak's Fifth Avenue 8

scrubwomen 13
secretaries 77
singing waiters 1
shoeshine lads 35
songs from World War I 29
spittoons 19
Staten Island buildings 51
Staten Island Ferry 1
Statue of Liberty 34
Stock Exchange 7
stock market crash 35
street debaters 1
street organs 19
street vendors 35
subways 13, 55, 78
Sullivan, John L. 23
songwriters' mall 29

T

Tavern On The Green 7
taxidrivers 5
theater 55, 64, 69
Times Square 10, 57
"Twenty One" ("21") 2

W

"wall art" 47
wartime music hall 29
wartime songs 29
Windsor, Kathleen 70
World War I 29, 30
World War II 40, 41, 51, 57
writers 49